The Basic Essentials of
CROSS-COUNTRY
SKIING

by
John Moynier

Illustrations by
Li Newton

ICS BOOKS, INC.
Merrillville, Indiana

THE BASIC ESSENTIALS OF CROSS-COUNTRY SKIING

recycled paper

All ICS titles are printed on 50% recycled paper from pre-consumer waste. All sheets are processed without using acid.

Published by:
ICS BOOKS, Inc.
1370 E. 86th Place
Merrillville, IN 46410
800-541-7323

Library of Congress Cataloging-in-Publication Data

Moynier, John
    Cross country skiing--the basic essentials of / by John Moynier ;
illustrations by Li Newton.
      p. cm.--(The Basic essentials series)
    Includes index.
    ISBN 0-934802-49-1 :
    1. Cross-country skiing.   I. Title.
GV855.3.M69 1990
796.93'2--dc20   90-41890
                                        CIP

TABLE OF CONTENTS

INTRODUCTION

Cross country skiing is the original form of winter recreation. Thousands of years ago, in the snowy lands of Scandanavia, people skied because it was the most efficient way to travel over the winter landscape. Today, that still holds true, but we also cross country ski for the pure pleasures of sport, exercise and enjoying the outdoors.

As those Nordic people moved to other lands, they took their beloved skis with them and introduced "nordic" skiing to the rest of the world. In fact, modern alpine or downhill skiing has its roots in cross country skiing and many folks still find that crossing over from one to the other increases their overall enjoyment of skiing.

As cross country skiing has grown as a form of winter recreation, the sport has naturally diversified and developed into a broad range of experiences. Most people think of cross country skiing as touring or day hiking on skis; but it is more than that. On one end of the spectrum there is the more aerobic track skiing and skating, citizen races and Olympic competitions. At the other end, are the thrills of downhill skiing on "skinny" skis, "telemarking" on the lifts and touring deep into the backcountry.

Watching a good skier gracefully telemark down a powder slope or effortlessly skate the local trails can be both inspiring and frustrating. As with any sport, more advanced skills come with time and practice. This book will introduce you to these skills, the next step is to take a lesson from a PSIA (Professional Ski Instructors of America) certified instructor at an established ski touring center. These pros can improve your skiing and show you new ways to have a safe and fun skiing experience.

Cross country skiing holds something for everyone. It's a great sport for the entire family. It can be as exciting, aerobic, fun or relaxing as you want it to be. Take some time, learn these skills and a whole world of winter recreation will open up for you. Soon you'll be enjoying the unique sensation of gliding over the snow and moving quietly through the beautiful winter landscape. Happy skiing!

THE QUIET PLEASURES OF TOURING

They had left the city that morning, but now they were in a quiet wilderness that seemed a world away. As their cross country skis glided through the sparkling new snow, they felt revitalised. At first they had talked about their jobs and commitments, but as they skied deeper into the forest, they no longer felt the need. Breathing in time with the strides of their skis, they quietly enjoyed the sounds of the forest.

Behind a tree, Jan surprised a snowshoe hare and it exploded from the snow in a cloud of glinting diamonds. They laughed at how they had almost skied over it; the rabbit had been so well camouflaged. As they toured on, they thought about their friends standing in line at the alpine resort. "I'll bet it's pretty crowded," Tim said to himself. Soon they reached the little knoll at the top of the trail. Below them stretched a gentle slope that opened through the trees and ended at the creek.

The view from the top was spectacular but the lure of the new powder soon turned their thoughts to the descent. Memories of their last trip brought a smile to Jan's face. "Remember that fall you took? You looked like Frosty the Snowman." Tim just laughed and started down the slope, gracefully linking telemarks through the untracked snow. Jan matched his turns, leaving a set of perfect figure eights and came to stop beside him.

"How about lunch?" Tim asked, although he guessed the answer. "Race you back to the top for another run," Jan replied. "I thought you were tired," he said. "Not anymore," she called over her shoulder as she headed back up the hill. "I'm glad we decided to go cross country skiing".

1. BALANCE

Freedom of the Heels

Cross country skiing to most folks invites an image of freedom. They can picture themselves gliding effortlessly through an untouched winter wilderness. Free to go where they choose, their skis provide a way to escape their everyday cares as well as crowded lift lines and expensive lift prices. It's a healthy way to spend a quiet day outdoors in winter.

A Question of Balance

It has often been said that if you can walk, you can cross country ski. The basic movements are the same and nordic skiing needn't take any more effort than walking around the block. However, as soon as our skis start to slide, we may feel like someone has iced the sidewalk. Obviously walking on a slippery street is very different from a dry one, and the first time on skis can sometimes feel like we've stepped on banana peels with both feet. Perhaps comparing skiing to learning to roller-skate might be a better example. Once we get used to the concept of sliding, we move from walking to skiing.

The addition of glide is what makes skiing so unique. If you've roller-skated, ice-skated or downhill skied, you've experienced glide and have developed your sense of balance to compensate for it. Balance is the key to glide.

The Flamingo

Have you ever wondered how a flamingo can sleep standing on one leg? Obviously they have a well developed, innate sense of balance, but think of their body position. Wings are tucked in and their weight is centered over the middle of their foot. We can develop that same good balance by working on our body position.

Try standing up straight in a good military (bad skiing) posture: knees locked, stomach in, chest out, shoulders back. In this stance we are easily tipped over. This is made worse if we raise our arms or move our head or hands. Now, relax and slouch like a kid trying to get out of going to grandma's. Relax from your toes up. Wiggle them. Flex your ankles and knees. Feel your weight move from your heels to your toes and settle it just back of the ball of your foot near the arch.

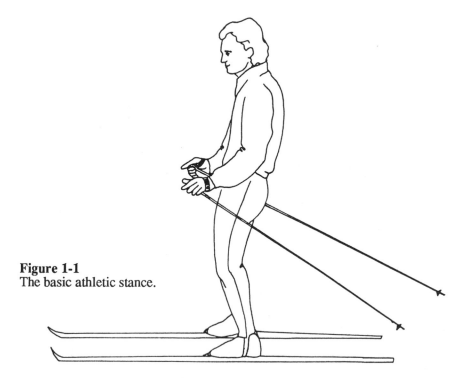

Figure 1-1
The basic athletic stance.

Relax your hips and press them forward, drawing your torso into a curve, with your shoulders cupped. Let your arms dangle and bring your hands up. Imagine you're carrying a tray or shopping bag. Your eyes should be looking forward, not at your feet. This is what we call the athletic stance. It's the basic body position for all your skiing.

Now, close your eyes and see if you can maintain your balance. Shift your center of gravity (basically your sternum) over one foot. Your nose, knee and toes will be aligned. In this position, you should be able to lift the other foot and balance like a sleeping flamingo. Keep your arms and hands still; any movement will throw you off. Work on this until you can balance on either foot. Now you're ready to try sliding on skis.

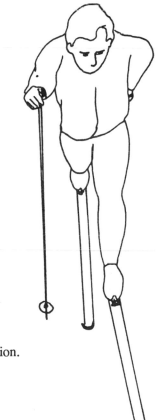

Figure 1-2
The "Flamingo" position.

2. THE BASIC STRIDE

Walk Don't Run

Let's go back to the idea of walking on skis. Most of us haven't thought about how to walk since we were kids. Maybe a review is in order. When we were kids, we shuffled our feet and mom yelled at us. Here it's okay. First, begin in your basic stance. Standing on one foot, shuffle forward with the other foot, stepping first on the heel. Transfer your weight onto that foot by bringing your hips forward, stepping off the ball/toe area of the other foot.

When we walk our arms naturally swing from the shoulders, matching the rhythm of our feet. Have you ever noticed that it's the opposite hand and foot that swing forward? It's the same in your skiing stride. Try to be natural and relaxed. If you think about it you'll start walking like a camel, with the same foot and hand swinging forward.

Figure 2-1
The basic stride.

As we noted, unless you're walking on an icy sidewalk, you normally don't have to worry about balance or traction. On skis you do. These long, skinny boards have a lot of spring under the foot. This is called the camber. When you step forward, push down, not back, to force the grip area of the ski base into the snow. This is called the "kick". Imagine you're trying to squash a big ugly bug with your foot.

When your weight transfers to the other foot, that ski will start to slide. Assume your balanced flamingo position again and ride it until it almost stops before you kick again. This is called the "glide". Kick and glide combine to form the basic stride. At this stage it may seem like you're shuffling around in oversized bedroom slippers.

You might have noticed that you also have really long poles. At first these are just used for balance, but you can use them to help you move forward, too. Adjust the straps so that they cradle your hands, freeing you from a tiring death grip and allowing you to pull on the straps for leverage.

If you take the natural pendulum arm swing from your normal walking stride and add the poles, you can pull on the straps as your arms swing back through the stride, propelling you forward. It's almost like pulling yourself on rope railings along the sides of the track. Relax. Poling can add power and momentum to your stride without much extra effort.

It's easiest to learn on flat terrain, like a meadow or frozen pond. However, as Columbus proved, the world isn't flat. Let's just concern ourselves now with the slightest ups and downs and get more comfortable on our skis. As we become more confident, we can tackle steeper terrain.

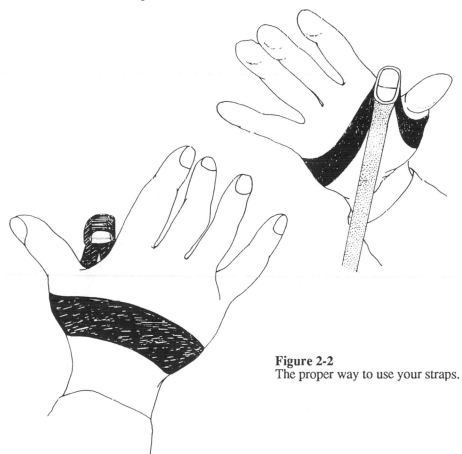

Figure 2-2
The proper way to use your straps.

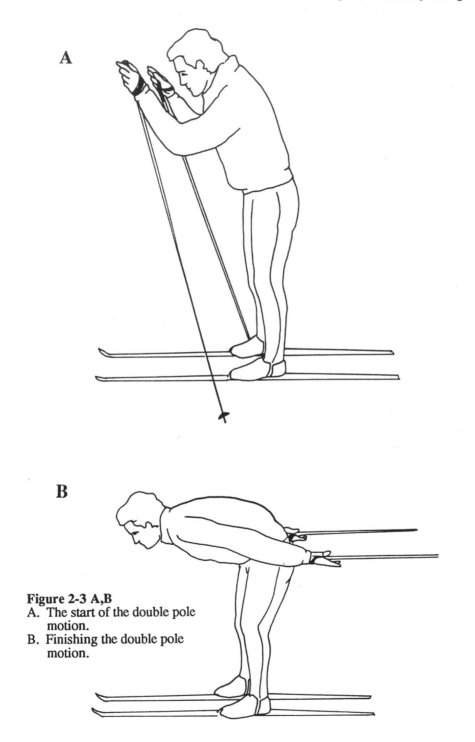

Figure 2-3 A,B
A. The start of the double pole motion.
B. Finishing the double pole motion.

Double Pole

There are times when it's more efficient to use just your poles, especially on slight downhills. You can gain a little speed and rest your legs as well. Practice hanging on the straps of both your poles. Keep your arms flexed and pull with your stomach and back muscles. Try not to use your arm muscles as much. As you hinge at the waist, your body weight will lever against the poles, propelling you forward. It almost feels like you're falling on the poles or that you're doing a sit-up.

To recover your poles for the next poling motion, swing your hands up. Bringing your hips back up and forward will help increase your glide. Try to keep looking down the track, not at your feet. A good double pole motion is vital to learning more advanced techniques like skating. Take the time to get comfortable with it. You can also add extra speed by kicking with one foot while you double pole. The timing is "kick, double pole". Armed with these basic techniques, you're now ready to explore the local woods and meadows.

3. BASIC DOWNHILL SKILLS

One Step At a Time

The time to learn how to deal with downhills is not at the top of the hill, but while you're on the flats. Turning is fun, once you get the knack; but it can be downright awkward at first with these long boards strapped to your feet. The key is don't try to do it all at once, take it one step at a time. First learn the movements while you're standing still, and then try them while your moving.

Star and Stepturns

These turns are simple ways to change the direction your skis are going. For the "star" turn, transfer all of your weight to one ski. Pick the tip of the other ski up by lifting your toes, knee and hip. Pushing down on your heel will keep the tails from crossing. By rotating your foot and knee out you can step the tip away from the other foot. Transferring your weight to that foot lets you pick up the other foot and match it. If you turn in a complete circle, your tracks will leave a star pattern in the snow. We call this a "star" turn.

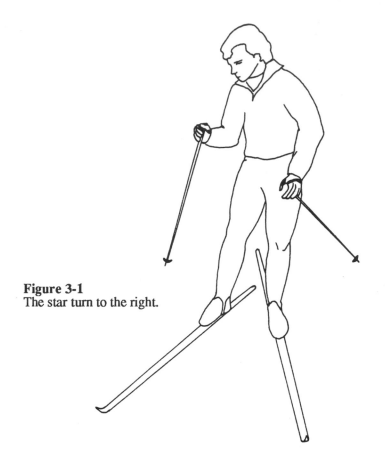

Figure 3-1
The star turn to the right.

We can use this same maneuver while we're sliding to step over or around an obstacle. This is called a "step turn". Take lots of little steps instead of a few big ones (it's easier to maintain your balance). By remembering to step with the ski in the direction you are going you can avoid an embarrassing cross-over. The step turn is a very important basic survival maneuver. You can step all the way across the hill until you come to a stop. Practicing it can also help you learn to skate.

Speed Control

It's possible to control your speed by making your skis into a wedge, pushing snow out of the way like a plow. Put all your weight on one ski again. Pick up the other ski slightly by lifting your heel, knee and hip. This will make the tail of the ski light.

Now pivot or twist that heel out so that the tail of the ski fans out into a half wedge. If you are in a groomed track you must pick the ski up out of the track first, and then move the tail out. By pressuring the edge of that ski, you will be able to brake by "shaving" off snow with the edge.

This is called the "one-ski wedge" and it's great for slowing down in prepared tracks. You can practice this on the flats by double poling hard to gain speed and then braking with one ski. P.S. Don't put too much weight on the wedged ski or it will cross over the other one.

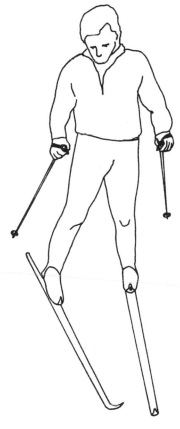

Figure 3-2
Moving the right ski out into a one ski wedge.

Gliding and Braking Wedge

If you are on a smooth slope, you can push both ski tails out to make a wedge or "snowplow". Keep the tips together and tails apart by rotating out with your heels. Try to keep your knees and ankles flexed for better balance. You can vary your speed by varying the size of your wedge. Keep your skis flat for a "gliding wedge" or edge them in with your feet and knees to produce a "braking wedge".

By pushing out the tails and edging hard with both skis you can come to a stop. If it's too steep, take your skis off and walk. It's often the best way down.

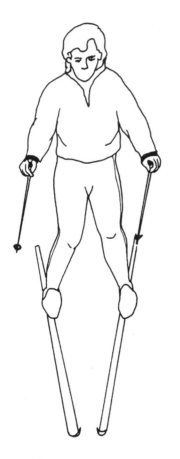

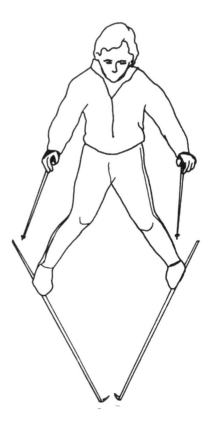

Figure 3-3
The gliding wedge.

Figure 3-4
The braking wedge.

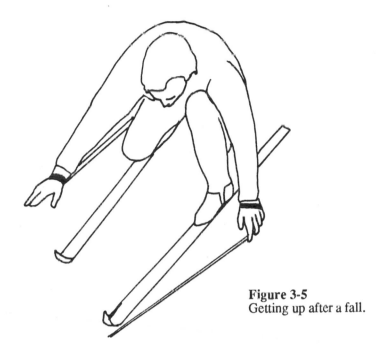

Figure 3-5
Getting up after a fall.

Getting Up

Everyone falls. Falling is not something to be ashamed of. In fact, think of it as a form of speed control. Sometimes the best way to slow down is to sit down. Be creative, but it's important to know how to get up before you get too creative. First, sort yourself out. Get your skis untangled and clean the snow out of your glasses. Scoot yourself around until your skis are below you and facing across the hill (if they point downhill at all they will start to slide when you stand up).

While resting on one hip, try to push the downhill ski ahead so that your heel is on the ski. Get up on the other knee and pretend to tie the forward boot's laces. You should now be able to stand up on that forward foot with a little push from your hands. If the snow is too deep, don't try to pull yourself up with your poles (you'll probably bend or break them). Make an "X" with your poles and push on the center. This will give you a better platform. Once you're on your skis, dust yourself off and admire your crater before heading off to try again.

4. CLASSIC TECHNIQUE

The Next Step
For many folks, the basic stride is all they need to know about cross country skiing. At this point the skis become tools to enable them to access the snowy winter trails. The shuffle takes minimal energy, practice and skill; but to really experience glide, we need to move on. The next step is the diagonal stride and other "classic" track techniques.

The Diagonal Stride
There is a subtle difference between the shuffle and a graceful diagonal stride. The goal is to produce a short burst of energy, the kick, and recover while you glide. It's primarily a matter of weight transfer. You can glide better by shifting your weight completely from ski to ski (remember that nose, knee and toes position). This will also give you a better position for your kick.

Try jogging on your skis. Feel your knees flex and spring. Your skis should get more traction as you stomp them into the snow. They won't glide as much, however, as the quicker tempo doesn't give them a chance. Now try mixing in a few slow motion strides with your jog steps. Feel the skis take off as you downshift your gears.

Ultimately we want to combine the kick of the jog step with the glide of the slow motion stride to produce the classic "diagonal stride". The name comes from the diagonal line created by your outstretched hand and opposite leg during the glide. Don't try to imitate this position, let it develop with time. It's a result of an aggressive body position rather than reaching with your hand or kicking your foot back.

As you transfer your weight to the new ski, try to bring your hip forward so your knee extends out over your toes, under your nose. As you finish your kick, lift your other hip over the gliding ski. This seemingly odd stance will effectively make the other leg shorter, giving it more clearance to swing through for the next kick.

Figure 4-1
The diagonal stride.

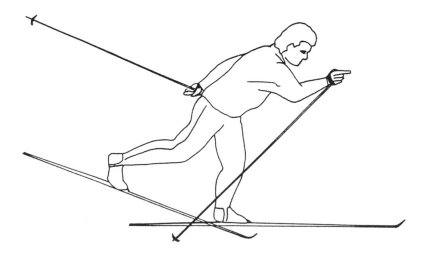

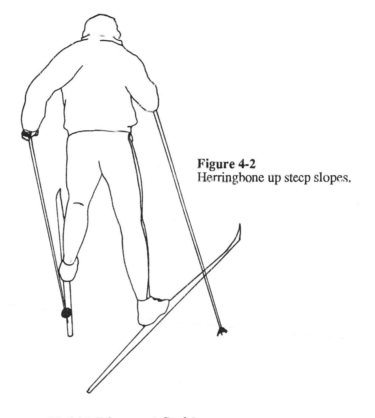

Figure 4-2
Herringbone up steep slopes.

Uphill Diagonal Stride

Steep uphills require a shorter, quicker stride to give you grip. In order to keep your weight over your feet, hinge your body at the hip. You should still feel the weight land on your heels as you transfer your weight in the stride. Pushing your feet up the hill will help. Really try to squash those bugs under your foot now. Your arm swing will be shortened also, keep your hands moving up the hill to add momentum.

Herringbone

On really steep uphills, your skis will eventually start to slip backwards. To combat this, splay the tips of your skis apart and step each ski up the hill, pressing on the inside edges of the skis. The steeper the hill, the wider the "V". The poles are again used to push you up the hill. The track left by this technique resembles a fish's ribs, thus the name "herringbone".

A

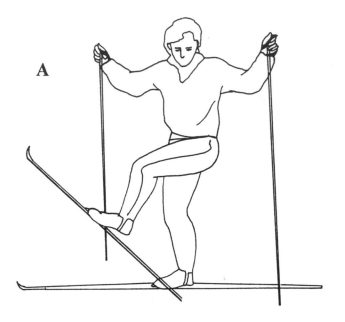

B

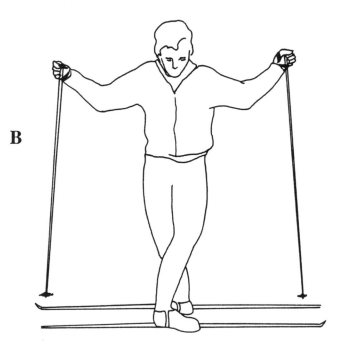

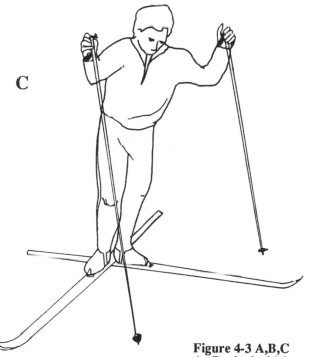

C

Figure 4-3 A,B,C
A. Begin the kick turn by stepping toward the turn.
B. Bring the lead ski along side the other ski.
C. Finish the kick turn by swinging the other ski around.

Sidestep and Kickturn

Some slopes are too steep to even herringbone. If you must get up these, then the sidestep is your best bet. It's exactly like it sounds. You can either step sideways straight up the hill or traverse uphill at an angle. Either way, there will come a time when you'll need to change directions. The slope is now too steep for a star turn and a "kick" turn is called for.

It helps to be flexible for effective kick turns. First, get your skis pointed across the slope. Now, decide which direction you're going to turn. On lower angle slopes, turning into the hill is easier; on steeper slopes, turning away is better (although more intimidating).

Use your poles for balance, opening your body to the turn like you're opening a door. Step with the ski in the direction you're turning. (A.) Try to get it all the way around so that it's parallel to the other ski. Your tips will now be going in opposite directions and your feet should be close together like a ballet dancer. (B.) Now move the other pole so that you can support yourself on it and swing around the other ski. (C.) When everything is facing the right way, off you go again. This is one of those tricks that seems impossible at first, but immediately gets easier with just a little practice.

5. LEARNING TO TURN

Don't LetThe Hills Get You Down

Downhills can be the most intimidating part of a ski tour until you master a few basic turns. The basic object is to control the speed and direction your skis are going. After a while, though, the thrill of linking turns becomes addictive and you'll be anxious to learn more fun and advanced ways to turn your skis.

Wedge Turn

First, let's go back to the gliding and braking wedge. When you feel comfortable with these maneuvers, you'll have a basic handle on edging and pressuring your skis. Now it's time to talk about steering. Steering is generated by rotating your feet, ankles, knees and hips through the turn. Both feet to the right for a right turn, to the left for a left turn. Make sense? The idea is to steer both your skis into every turn.

As you begin in a gliding wedge, try to rotate or steer both tips towards the turn. If the skis are flat this will be easier. As you gradually turn across the hill, more of your weight will be pulled

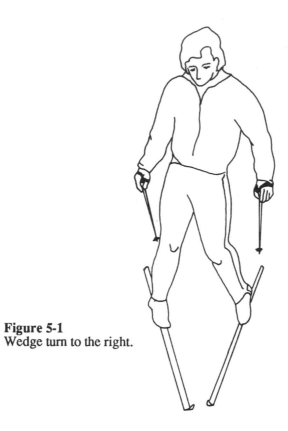

Figure 5-1
Wedge turn to the right.

onto the downhill or "outside" ski. That's great! Edge that ski a bit and pressure it to help finish the turn. Sinking your weight on this ski by flexing your knees and ankles will help even more. It may sound confusing, but weighting the left ski will turn you right and weighting the right will turn you left. Right?

To make the next turn, stand up tall and steer both your tips down the hill. Keep steering them until you feel more pressure build up on the new outside ski. Pressuring that foot will now finish the turn. The big toe/arch side of that foot will get most of the weight while the inside foot will get light. This will begin to feel like pedaling a bike with weight increasing from one foot to the other as you go from turn to turn. Voila! With a little practice you'll be linking turns down the hill and ready to tackle more advanced skills.

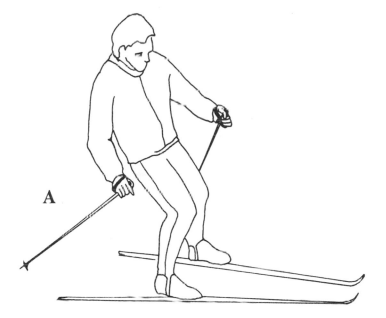

Figure 5-2 A,B,C
A. Begin a wedge christy by rising
into the turn.

Wedge Christies

The term "christy" is short for Christiana, the region in Norway where this maneuver originated. The idea is to skid your skis a bit through the turn to slow your speed. Breathe in as you rise into the turn, letting your skis drift sideways a little and then edge them as you breathe out to finish the turn. Because your skis stay light at the beginning of the turn, it's easier to keep them closer together. In fact, as soon as you feel the outside ski start to get more weight, try to steer the unweighted inside ski back parallel to the outside ski so that you finish the turn with your skis together.

To get into the next turn, rise up and look downhill with your upper body. (A.) Point your outside hipbone down the hill and stand tall on that ski. This will help flatten and unweight your skis. Your lower body will want to rotate with your torso, thus helping to initiate the steering of your skis into the turn. (B.) Finish the

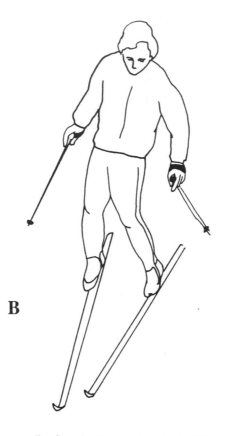

B

B. Stand tall and steer both skis
   into the turn.

turn by sinking your weight onto the outside ski. (C.) Don't let
your weight fall back onto the inside ski; this will cause you to slip
out at the finish of your turn.

   Soon, you will develop a rhythm of "rise and steer, sink and
match", transferring your weight from ski to ski. Stand tall into the
turn, small to finish. This up and down motion forms the basis of
weighting and unweighting that will continue into telemark and
parallel turns. Remember, all turns result from a combination of
steering, pressuring and edging your skis. The differences come
mainly with speed and changes in snow conditions.

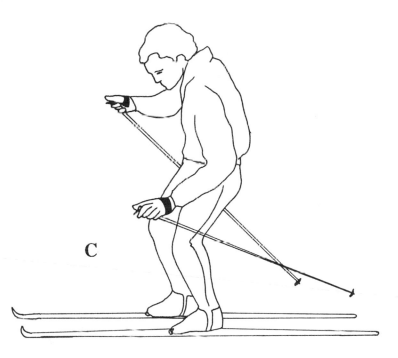

C. Finish the turn by sinking and
matching the inside ski.

The faster you go on the snow, the easier turns get. Speed is your ally, although at first it may seem like your enemy. Smaller turns that keep your skis pointing more downhill are much easier than big round turns that tour all over the slope. Learn to be comfortable looking down the hill. This is called facing the "fall-line" (the line a snowball would roll down the hill). Keeping your upper body looking down the fall-line is very important to more advanced skiing and gives you much quicker and more positive turns.

6. BASIC SKATING TECHNIQUES

Skating Away

Skating is a really fun and exciting way to ski. For many folks, learning to skate is easier and more natural than learning the diagonal stride. Most of us have skated at some time in our lives and we can draw on that experience. Skating is faster than classic technique, but it also puts more energy demands on the skier. Trying to skate in new snow can be quite tiring, but when conditions are right, skating can feel like flying.

The Diagonal Skate

The easiest way to learn to skate is to take your diagonal stride out of the tracks. At first it will seem a bit awkward and you might have trouble recovering your ski tips. Try practicing your step turns again to get used to controlling your skis. Adding a push off the edges of your skis will turn your step turns into "skate" turns, too.

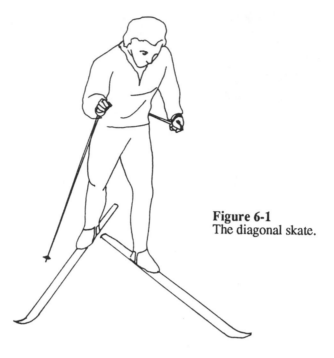

Figure 6-1
The diagonal skate.

Another easy way to trick yourself into skating is to add glide to your herringbone. Waddle over a short hill and continue onto the flats. Remember how you used the "nose, knees, toes" position for better glide in the diagonal? Well, it really helps in skating. Try to get your hip up and over the gliding ski on each side. This will also help your balance.

The next step is to tip your skis on their edge as you glide. If you push off that edge onto the next gliding ski you'll have a better platform and will have begun to skate. The poles are used just like the diagonal stride, thus the name "diagonal" skate. Racers use this technique on the steepest uphills for a super quick tempo.

"V" Skating

Figuring out the different skating maneuvers can be needlessly confusing. Later on we'll look at the specific techniques and applications, but for now let's just think of "V" skating as adding a double pole motion to our basic skate.

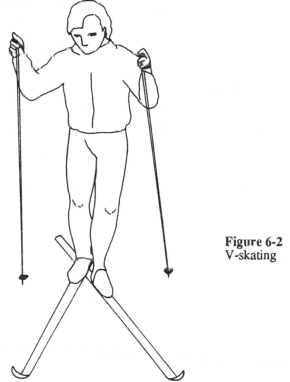

Figure 6-2
V-skating

Let's go back to the double pole. We're now using slightly longer poles than for our classic skiing and this gives us more push. Some folks feel more comfortable double poling every time they skate. This is what downhill skiers do to get from lift to lift. Other folks prefer a strong side and only pole on that side. Either way, it's important to remember that we're now double poling while gliding on one ski instead of two.

Practice this in the tracks and see how well you can balance on one ski while poling. See how many double pole pushes you can get in before you have to weight the other foot. Don't forget the "nose, knee, toes" position for better balance.

Now try double poling on one ski out of the tracks. You'll soon find if you prefer poling on one or both sides. If you notice your ski tips splaying apart, don't fight it. Add in a small skate to recover the ski. If your skis slip sideways, think of edging them in with your ankles and arch. Having a strong double pole and good one-ski balance are very important. As we'll see, there are many pole timing variations, but for now, just enjoy skating.

Skating Practice

Practice skating without your poles. You'll need to push off the edges of the skis to get anywhere. Try bending your knees and extending them in an exagerated kick like a speed skater. You can also swing your hands to generate additional momentum. Humming a skating tune will help develop a fun, comfortable rhythm.

To practice balance, see how few skates it takes you to cover a given distance. The trick is getting that flamingo body position, lining up over the gliding ski. You'll be surprised at how much more efficient this will make your skating. To practice edging, try pushing a partner along ahead of you in the tracks while you skate behind them. It may look funny, but it's a fun way to improve your skating.

Whether you push with one pole or two, one side or both; it's most important to get a good feel for the edging, kick and glide of the basic skating motion. Then you can get tricky and try different pole timings.

7. LEARNING TO PARALLEL AND TELEMARK

Yo-Yo Skiing

Now we are getting into the realm of "nordic downhill". Often these maneuvers are most easily learned on the "bunny" slopes at a downhill ski area. Ride up, ski down: just like a yo-yo. You'll get in more mileage and progress faster. This is especially true if you can take a lesson or are able to ski with better skiers.

Parallel Turns

While parallel turns might seem to be the realm of the downhill skier, we can do them too. In fact, it's easier to learn to telemark if you know the basics of the parallel turn. A parallel is really not that different from a wedge christy, we just keep our skis together throughout the turn instead of initiating with a wedge. This parallel position gives us good lateral or side-to-side stability which is useful is bracing ourselves against gravity on firm snow.

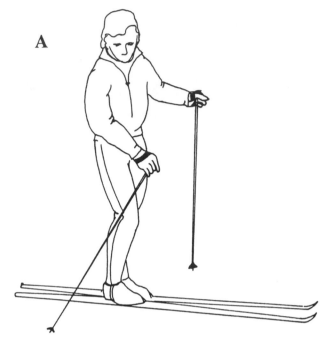

Figure 7-1 A,B
A. Stand tall and steer into the
   parallel turn.
B. Finish the parallel by sinking
   onto the outside ski.

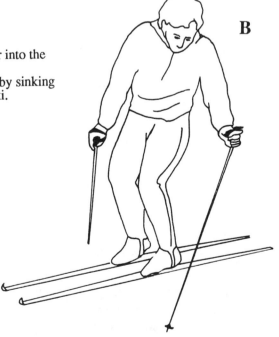

Now it's really important to face downhill with your hips and torso to initiate a turn. Feel the weight shift to the outside ski as you begin to rise up and steer both skis downhill. Because your inside ski gets light right away, it's easy to keep it close and parallel throughout the turn. Relax your body and remember to rise into the turn, sink out of it.

Learning to plant your pole can help you develop a rhythm. Just flick your downhill wrist so that the basket touches the snow, downhill of your skis as you start the next turn. The timing is "tap, turn; tap, turn". Let the pole follow you though the turn.

Telemark Turns

The telemark is the badge of honor for most cross country skiers. Developed in the Telemark region of Norway, it is the goal of almost all skinny skiers. It's really not that different from the parallel, except that we lead with the outside ski. In the backcountry, the telemark is useful to gain fore-and-aft stability, especially in deep or changeable snow. We do this at the expense of lateral stability, however, so be forewarned.

To begin with, we need to learn the telemark position. This is the first real variation on our athletic stance. First get into the "flamingo" position, standing on one foot. Now feel all the weight move slightly forward onto the ball of that foot. Next, shuffle forward with the other foot so that there is a little pressure on that heel. So far, this is similar to the basic stride.

Where it differs, though, is that you don't take the weight off that back foot. By flexing your ankles, knees and hips forward, you sink down into the telemark position with your weight on both feet. To go into the next position, stand up over that forward foot, weight on the ball and shuffle forward with the rear foot; sinking into the new, equal weighted position.

You can practice this maneuver down a very gentle slope. This exaggerated stride will also help you learn the rhythm of the telemark as well as the lead change. You won't have much balance side-to-side, so you can cheat by dragging your poles as outriggers to give yourself more stability. Don't stab the snow with your poles, keep your hands quiet and low.

Figure 7-2
Sink your weight onto both skis for
the telemark position.

To turn from this position, use the same movements as in your
other turns, but remember the outside ski will be leading. As you
rise into a new telemark position, you will be unweighting your
skis. At this point, steer both skis into the turn (away from the
leading ski) and begin to edge them. Instead of shifting all your
weight to the outside ski, remember to keep weight on the inside
ski. Feeling pressure on the little toe of the rear foot will remind
you of this and will help keep the trailing ski on the inside edge.

As desirable as the telemark turn is, learning the telemark
position is much more important. Practicing the telemark stride
down a gentle slope will help develop good body position and
proper weighting as well as refine the lead changes which are
unique to the telemark. Soon you'll be gracefully turning down
slopes you've only dreamed of before.

Figure 7-3
Stand tall and steer both skis into
the turn.

8. ADVANCED SKATING TECHNIQUES

Skating On Thin Ice

Well, now we get onto the thin ice of definitions. Modern skating has progressed to where there are now many specific techniques and applications for the terrain found at a touring center or race course. These are mainly pole timing variations. It can seem pretty subtle, but if you're interested in racing and advanced skating, you'll need these different techniques.

Marathon Skating

Marathon skating was the first skating technique to be widely used on the international race scene. It makes use of a groomed track and can be most closely compared to adding a one legged skate to your double pole. It's used mostly for very fast terrain.

The timing is "pole and skate, glide", with the weight transfer beginning with the start of the double pole. How much weight you transfer depends on the snow conditions. Keep a narrow "V" with your skate and transfer more weight for hard snow, less for softer conditions.

Figure 8-1
The marathon skate keeps one ski
in the tracks.

V-1 Skating

V-1 skating is used for moderately steep uphills. Edging and tempo are more important than powerful poling. The timing of the poling is critical to a quick tempo. In the V-1, the double pole occurs on one side only and the poles are planted at the same time as you skate. The poles are recovered as the weight is skated back to the other ski, creating a "pole and skate, skate" timing.

When using this technique on very steep hills, increase your tempo and try to step up the hill with your feet. Your hands will reach up the hill, but they won't follow through as much. On extremely steep trails, racers may even use a "jump V-1".

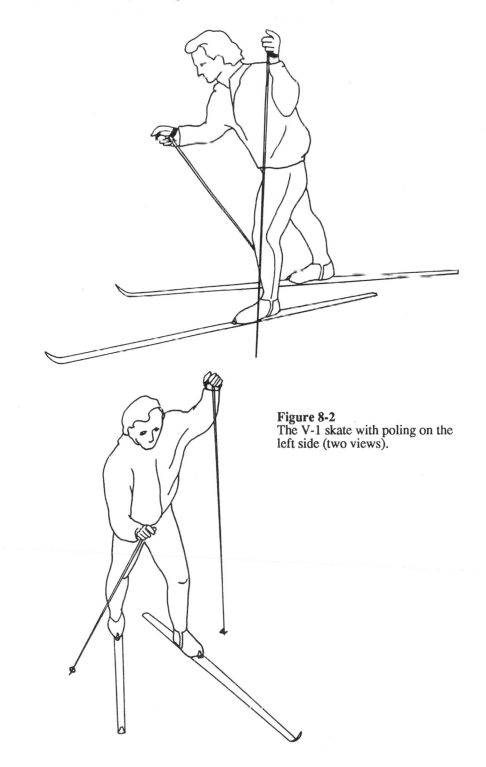

Figure 8-2
The V-1 skate with poling on the
left side (two views).

V-2 Skating

V-2 skating is very powerful as you get to push with both poles before every skate. Racers use this technique for very fast flats and slight downhills. In this technique there is a separation in the timing of the poling and skating. First you pole, then you skate. It's exactly like doing a double pole over one ski, then skating over to the other ski and repeating the process. "Pole, skate; pole, skate" is the mantra for the V-2.

V-2 Alternate Skating

If you find that it's too hard to recover in time to pole on both sides in the V-2, don't worry. Instead of poling again, swing your poles back to recover onto the gliding ski. Racers began using this technique at the end of long races when they were too tired to

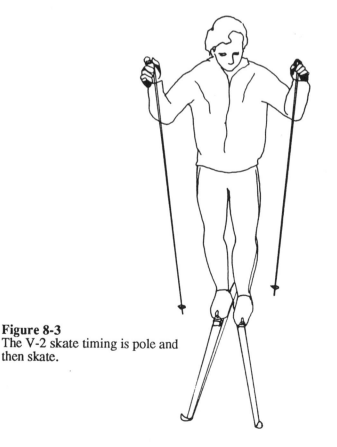

Figure 8-3
The V-2 skate timing is pole and
then skate.

balance well. This "pole, skate, swing" timing is really fast and rhythmic. Some folks confuse this with the V-1, but the timing is more like the V 2. Think of it as a V-2 with a pole swing replacing the second pole push, thus the name "V-2 Alternate".

No Poles Skating

You don't really drop your poles for this technique, but hold them up and swing them for more momentum. This technique is used on the fastest downhills. At these speeds there just isn't enough time to pole and a more aerodynamic stance is more efficient. At terminal velocity just drop into a tuck and hang on for dear life.

9. ADVANCED NORDIC DOWNHILL TECHNIQUES

Get Down With Style

There are as many variations to the basic telemark and parallel turns as there are skiers. Each of us will develop our own style and tricks to use when the going gets rough. Each turn may require a different technique depending on the snow conditions. It's all skiing, being creative only adds to the fun. As long as you maintain a good body position, you'll be fine.

Advanced Parallel

Whole books have been written on the refinement of alpine parallel techniques. It all boils down to using what works for the given snow condition. In deep powder, unweight your skis and steer them both at the same time. Unweighting occurs with a sinking motion combined with pulling your knees towards your chest. Rotate the tips towards the turn and finish by weighting both skis equally. Too much weight on one ski will cause it to sink.

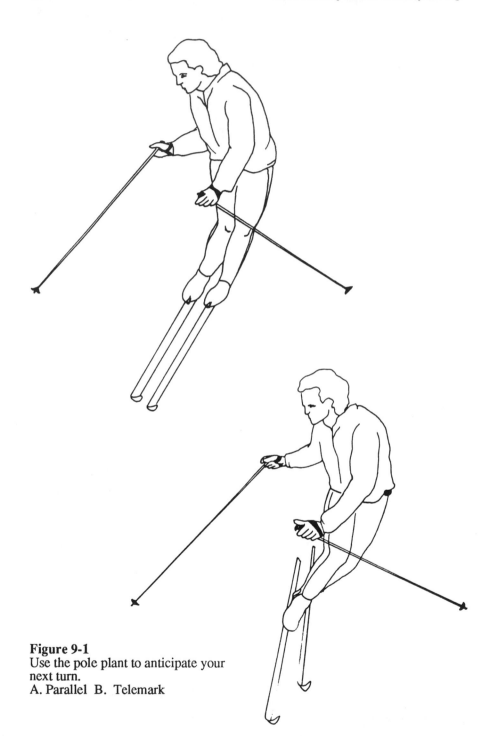

Figure 9-1
Use the pole plant to anticipate your
next turn.
A. Parallel B. Telemark

On firmer snow, commit all your weight to the outside ski very early in the turn. You may even skate into the turn, accelerating like a racer. On super steeps, you may be forced to jump your skis across the fall-line, almost coming to a stop with every turn.

Advanced Telemark Turns

There are many ways to initiate the telemark. You can go from the telemark stride, a wedge, or even hop into the position. The classic telemark for deep snow is similar to the telemark stride. Steer both skis into the turn as you unweight the skis. Try to keep both skis weighted equally. Otherwise, the lead ski will sink and you'll end up on your nose.

On firmer snow, stem one ski out to initiate the turn, transfer your weight to it, and then match with the inside ski. This more sequential initiation is especially good for breakable crusts as you can "test the water" before committing to the turn. On steeps, hop the outside ski across the fall-line and immediately follow with the inside ski in a two-step maneuver. The more you experiment with these techniques, the more fun you'll have when you venture into the backcountry.

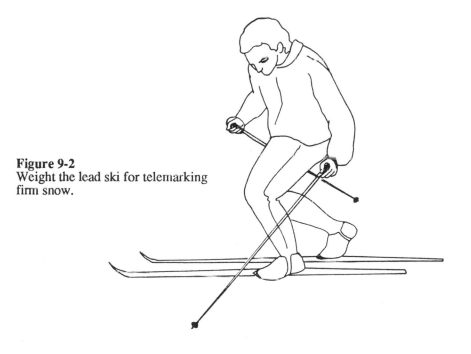

Figure 9-2
Weight the lead ski for telemarking
firm snow.

10. EQUIPMENT

Gearing Up

As with many sports, cross country skiing does require some specific equipment (it's pretty hard to go skiing without skis). The basic package is skis, boots, bindings and poles. As the sport has diversified, so has the gear. Today we may use a different set of gear to go skating or striding, touring or turning.

Touring Vs Turning

Cross country skis are designed to go across country. They have to grip well going uphill, glide on the flats and turn going downhill. They have two main characteristics built into them to help accomplish this: camber and flex.

Camber is the bow or spring built into the ski. Cross country skis are often said to have a "double camber". There aren't really two cambers, the ski is just stiffer right under the foot. This area is called the "kick" zone. The camber keeps the wax or waxless pattern in the kick zone off the snow for less friction while you're gliding. The tips and tails of the ski are always in contact with the snow, therefore they're called the "glide" zone. We can refer to the amount of camber a ski has as its "touring" characteristic. "Classic" racing skis have a very stiff "double" camber for maximum kick and glide. Touring skis have a light camber that flattens out under your body weight for better traction. Telemark skis may have almost no camber, making them more like downhill skis.

Flex is the force it takes to reverse the bow of the ski, either over the entire length or in a specific area like the tip or tail. When we turn our skis, we put them on edge and force them into an arc which they follow on the snow. The rounder the arc, the easier it is to turn. Flex therefore can be referred to as the "turning" characteristic of a ski.

Most telemark skis have a smooth, even flex. Softer flex allows easier turning in deep snow or slower speeds and provides a more

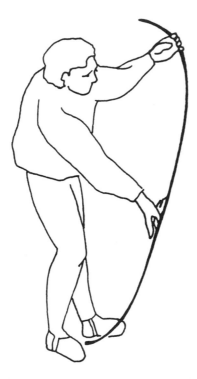

Figure 10-1
Checking ski flex.

"forgiving" ski. Stiffer flex is better for firmer snow or higher speeds and creates a more "responsive" ski. Most telemark skis will have sharp steel edges and a pronounced "sidecut" (wider tips and tails than the waist) to aid in turning on firmer snow.

Touring skis combine soft flex and double camber. Some have a metal edge for security on crusty snow, most don't as the edge adds weight and stiffness. Skating skis have an even flex, but a stiff camber. They turn better than striding skis which are flexed more like a hunting bow.

Choosing the right ski for you will then be a matter of weighing the touring versus turning characteristics of a ski and matching it to the type of skiing you expect to do. A light touring ski without a metal edge is probably the most versatile choice for a ski, as it will handle the widest range of ski experiences.

Traditionally, we size our skis by having the tip reach our wrist when our arm is stretched over our head. This will match the camber to your body weight if you are an average weight for your height. Folks who are light for their height should size 5-10 cm shorter. Heavier folks may choose a slightly longer ski. Skating and telemark skis can be sized like downhill skis (i.e. shorter skis are more maneuverable, longer skis go faster). When you're learning to skate or turn, try a shorter ski at first. Of course, renting skis is an economical and efficient way to find the ski which works best for you.

Waxless Vs Waxable

Cross country skis need some way to gain traction as they move across the flats or uphills. Most do this either by having a waxless pattern cut into the base or by applying a grip wax to the kick zone.

Waxing your skis for grip can be a rewarding or frustrating experience depending on the conditions and your experience. Most folks starting out prefer the ease of waxless skis.

A well waxed ski will usually out perform a waxless ski, but sometimes it's hard to wax your skis right. Conditions may change in an hour or around the next corner. Waxless skis will always work to some extent but you can't fine tune them. The term "waxless" is also something of a misnomer. All skis need to be waxed in the glide zone. This is usually done by "hot waxing" in a

A   **B**

Figure 10-2 A,B
A. Fitting ski length.
B. Fitting pole length.

glide wax into the base with an iron, then scraping off the excess wax. This will make them glide better and keep them from icing up.

Boots and Bindings

Most touring boots still use the traditional "3 pin" or "75-mm" binding. These bindings are 75-mm across the toe and use three pins and a bail to hold the toe in the binding. Increasingly, however, we are seeing more boot-binding systems being used. This is especially true in track skiing and skating. The most popular today are the Salomon Profil and the Rottefella NNN. Competing with the 3-pin is the new NNN-BC touring binding and others are on the way.

When choosing a boot, it's important to consider which type of binding you will want to use. The boot must fit your foot comfortably and perform to your needs. A skating boot is not appropriate for a backcountry tour and a telemark boot is cumbersome in the tracks. The NNN-BC is probably the most versatile system on the market.

Poles

Traditional cross country poles are used to give you push through the length of your stride. They are sized by fitting into the pit of your outstretched arm. For skating, we use poles that are 5-10 cm longer (up to your shoulders or chin). This gives you more leverage, but can be awkward at first. For off-track touring, choose a pole 5-10 cm shorter. Adjustable length poles are a good alternative, but are usually more expensive.

11. WINTER SAFETY

Be Prepared

Even though most of our skiing may be close to the car or touring center, we need to be prepared for changes in the weather, an accident or even getting lost. Remember, it is winter and even on a sunny day the temperature can be well below freezing. Blowing snow or a storm can turn any trip into a survival situation if you're not prepared. Avalanche and hypothermia awareness should be a part of every backcountry skiers' education.

Winter Weather

Be aware of the weather. Not just what will it do today, but tomorrow, too. What about yesterday? Be alert for changes and know when to turn around if a storm is approaching. Understanding winter weather patterns can make your skiing safer and more enjoyable, too. Wind chill can play a large roll in your comfort. Frostbite can catch you offguard and hypothermia has long been considered the "killer of the unprepared". Sunburn can be just as uncomfortable as cold. Remember, the snow will reflect the sun up under your chin and sunglasses and can cause "snow blindness" or sunburn of the eyes.

First Aid

Even if you always ski at a touring center with a ski patrol, it's important to have a basic knowledge of first aid, especially for cold injuries. Your local Red Cross will have classes and more information. Someone in your party should have a good first aid kit. In addition to basics like bandages, aspirin and antiseptic, commercially available hand-warmers work wonders and are easily carried.

Stretching is a great way to warm up and avoid injuries. Take the time to loosen up before skiing hard. Know your limits, too. "Be Aware, Ski with Care" is a national program for skier safety. Don't ski a trail you're not ready for, no matter what your friends say.

Routefinding

If you venture off of maintained trails, you need good routefinding skills. Choose a familiar route if you can, places where you've gone in the summer. There probably won't be any signs of a trail when it's buried in snow.

Picking the best route is not just a matter of being good with a map and compass. You should find a route that limits your exposure to the weather and avalanche hazard. The route should be well within each person's skiing ability. The top of a bowl is no time to learn that someone can't snowplow. Be careful of creek crossings and dense timber with heavily laden branches. Cross country skiing can be a lot of fun, but remember that winter weather can quickly make routefinding a lot more difficult.

Clothing and Accessories

Layering is the best way to dress warm for skiing. A wicking style thermal underwear should be the base layer. Sweaters, parkas or a windbreaker can be added or put in a pack as the day goes on. Knickers are the traditional nordic pants, but stretch tights have become more popular. Wind pants are a good addition for downhills and cooler days. Wool socks and hats are still the best choice for staying warm. It's easy to overdress for nordic skiing, it's better to work to stay warm than sweat.

Gaiters are essential. They keep snow from getting into your boot and protect your boots from wear. Gloves or mittens are also essential. Sunglasses and sunscreen are vital for protection from the sun and wind. A daypack or fanny pack is handy for storing your lunch, water and first aid kit as well as extra layers of clothes.

12. PRACTICE

Learning to ski better takes practice. You won't learn to telemark or skate on your first day out. Learning new skills is best reinforced with mileage. As you become proficient at a skill, you can build on that to learn another. All skiing is just pressure, steering, edging and balance. The difference between a beginning and advanced skier is the ability to do all of these at the same time. That takes practice. Skiing with better skiers is a great way to improve. Watching good skiers or videos is a good way to develop a positive mental image of these techniques.

Touring Centers

The best place to practice is at an established touring center. In addition to offering lessons, rentals and a warm day lodge; a touring center will have groomed trails to practice your skating, striding and hill skills. You can find a touring center near you through the Cross Country Ski Areas of America (CCSAA).

Lessons

There is no substitute for learning from a professional. Your friends may be helpful and have a lot of suggestions, but you will learn quicker from an experienced instructor. They will have a developed progression for all these maneuvers and can help make you more comfortable with their fun, innovative approaches.

Find an instructor who has been certified by the Professional Ski Instructors of America (PSIA). There are two levels of certification. Associate Certified Instructors are qualified to teach lessons up through intermediate skills. Full Certified Instructors are qualified to teach even the most advanced skills. Video analysis of your lesson is sometimes available and is a fun way to visualize your own skiing.

Just Do It

There's nothing like skiing to make you a better skier. The more you improve, the more you'll enjoy it. Winter is a magical time. It's ephemeral. You can't go skiing all year long unless you travel to the southern hemisphere. Savor it. Learn the pleasures of early season snow, mid-winter powder and spring corn. Soon you'll find yourself anticipating the first frost of fall and rejoice at the first snows of winter. Cross country skiing is a sport that can be enjoyed by people of all ages and all levels of motivation and fitness. I hope this book will help you discover the many joys of cross country skiing.

APPENDIX

Alpine skiing: using ski lifts at a ski resort
Athletic stance: the basic relaxed, body postion for skiing
Avalanche: uncontrolled movement of loose or cohesive snow
Basic stride: shuffling steps on skis
Bindings: the attachment points for the boots on the ski
Boards: slang for skis
Boots: specialized shoes for cross country skiing
Boot-binding systems: compatible clip attachments
Braking wedge: Wide, edged position used to slow speed
Camber: the bow built into the length of the ski
Christy: type of turn which uses skidding to control speed
Citizen races: informal nordic races for the public
Classic technique: maneuvers involving the diagonal stride
Crater: slang for the hole in the snow created by falling
Diagonal skate: skating with one pole at a time
Diagonal stride: movement combining kick and glide
Double pole: using both poles to move forward on skis
Downhill skiing: using ski lifts at a ski resort
Edging: tilting the ski on edge to control speed or turn
Fall-line: the line a snowball would roll down the hill
Flex: the amount of force it takes to reverse the ski's bow
Forgiving skis: easy to turn and absorb terain variations

Frostbite: tissue damage caused by exposure to cold or wind
Glide: overcoming friction by sliding on one or both skis
Glide wax: temperature graded wax which enhances glide
Glide zone: the tips and tails of the ski base
Gliding wedge: Narrow wedge for controlling speed
Gravity: primary physical force we all are slaves to
Groomed trails: machine prepared tracks and skating lanes
Half wedge: speed control position with one ski stemmed out
Herringbone: technique for going up very steep slopes
Hot waxing: ironing glide wax into the base of a ski
Hypothermia: lowering of body core temperature
Icing up: freezing of water in the pores of the ski base
Initiate: to begin a turn or movement
Inside ski: ski that is closer to the center of the turn
Jog step: exaggerated stride caused by jogging on skis
Jump V-1: very aggressive skate maneuver on hills
Kick: flattening the ski with the foot and knee to get grip
Kick-double pole: adding a kick to the double pole
Kick turn: 180 degree turn on the flats or a steep slope
Kick wax: temperature graded wax which provides grip
Kick zone: the section of the ski base under the foot
Leading ski: ski that is forward at the beginning of a turn
Lifts: chairs or gondolas at a ski area
Linked turns: moving from one turn to another without a stop
No-poles skate: swinging the poles for more momentum
Nose, knee, toes: basic body position for glide
Outside ski: ski that is away from the center of the turn
Parallel: body position used to gain lateral stability
Parallel turn: family of turns with feet close together
Pole plant: using the pole or poles for timing or push
Pole timing: directing the tempo with the pole plant
Poles: specialized ski poles for nordic skiing
Powder: Newly fallen snow of very light density
Pressure: adding weight to a ski for more control
Push off: kick or skate motion
Recovery: usually returning hands or skis to start position
Responsive skis: quick reacting, transmiting forces to skier
Shuffle: walking motion caused by scuffing the feet
Sidecut: difference between the tip, waist and tail widths
Sidestep: sideways technique for climbing steep slopes
Skating: using nordic skis to skate on snow
Skidding: gradual edging to control speed
Skinny skis: slang for cross country skis
Skis: the boards we slide on the snow with

Snow blindness: sunburn of the eyes
Snowplow: slang for braking wedge position
Spring corn: melt freze snow which is delightful to ski on
Steering: rotational force used to turn skis
Star turn: stationary step turn
Step turn: Maneuver used to step over or around obstacles
Stem: one ski steered into a half wedge
Stride: a forward step
Striding: using classic technique
Swing: swinging the hands to recover the body over a ski
Tail: rear end of the ski
Telemark: body position used to gain forward stability
Telemark stride: moving down a hill in telemark positions
Telemark turn: family of turns with outside ski leading
Telemarking: slang of the subsport of nordic downhill skiing
Tempo: the time used to cycle through one stride or skate
Tip: forward part of the ski (also called the shovel)
Touring: skiing off groomed trails, usually for the day
Touring center: ski area with groomed and marked trails
Track skiing: skiing in grooves cut into the snow
Tuck: aerodynamic body position for downhills
Unweighting: removing weight from the skis
V-skating: skating with both feet and both poles
V-1 skate: poling on one side only, at same time as skate
V-2 skate: double poling on both sides, before the skate
V-2 alternate: double poling on one side, before the skate
Waist: middle section of the ski
Weight transfer: moving your weight from one foot to another
Waxless pattern: a pattern cut into the kick zone for grip
Waxless skis: skis which use a waxless pattern for grip
Weighting: adding weight to the skis
Wicking: movement of moisture away from the skin
Yo-yo skiing: riding the lifts or climbing up to ski down
3-pin: binding which mates pins with holes in the boot
75-mm: standard cross country binding width for touring

INDEX